AF251951

Leanna

Killer Whales

Killer whales are found in oceans all over the world, especially in cooler waters and polar regions. The killer whale is the largest member of the dolphin family and is also called an Orca whale. It can swim as fast as 30 miles per hour and is the fastest in the dolphin family.

The easily recognized dorsal fin of the male can be as tall as 6 feet and is straight. The female's fin curves or hooks toward the back and is less than 3 feet tall. Killer whales grow to lengths of 20 to 30 feet and weigh between 9,000 and 14,000 pounds.

Although there are many myths about killer whales, they do not attack people. The name killer whale comes from the fact they are very good hunters and eat massive amounts of food because they are so big.

Killer whales are social animals that hunt, play and travel together in the same group, called pods. Pods are made up of males, females and young whales, and have an average of 30 members. These whales live for 30 to 50 years, and usually stay with the same pod for life.

Discover Killer Whales
The Long Journey North

Written by Debi Buettner
Illustrated by Kim Branson and Jason Karecki

The winter morning fog begins to lift along the coast of Oregon. Out in the ocean, a pod of killer whales slowly rises to the water's surface. Their tall black dorsal fins rise higher and higher out of the water. Some of the fins are taller than a grown man. Whoosh! The huge whales spout gusts of steam from their blowholes. After they take a fresh breath, they quickly dive back underwater.

Suddenly the pod crashes through the surface, and in unison, the whales gracefully leap high in the air. They twist their smooth black and white bodies, and then land on their sides, making huge loud splashes that can be heard for miles. This is called breaching. Whales do this to see where they are or as a form of play. Sometimes the loud splash is used to communicate with other whales that are nearby.

As they return to the water, some of the whales slap the surface with their tails. A few of the young, called calves, appear to be playing as they continue to leap and dive. Most of the adults are resting on the surface. A glint of sunlight shows off the saddle, or gray marking, behind one whale's dorsal fin.

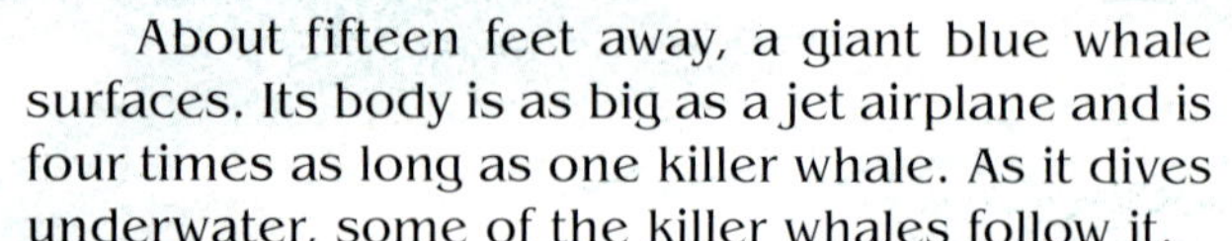

About fifteen feet away, a giant blue whale surfaces. Its body is as big as a jet airplane and is four times as long as one killer whale. As it dives underwater, some of the killer whales follow it.

From a distance, they watch the torpedo-shaped whale take in a big gulp of water then filter it out.

The blue whale is a baleen whale and does not have teeth like killer whales. Instead, it has a baleen, which is like a large fringed brush that hangs down from the top of its mouth. The baleen traps or catches any food in the water. The killer whales watch the massive blue whale for a few minutes, then return to the surface.

A short while later, three females dive underwater to help a mother while she has a baby. As soon as it is born, the mother and her helpers nudge the newborn toward the surface. The baby swims on his own to the surface for his first breath of air. His rubbery feeling skin is black and orange, but will soon change to black and white, like the skin of the adult whales.

One of the males, called a bull, dives and sends out clicking noises using echolocation. The clicks bounce off objects in front of the whale and send back signals, like echoes. Whales also use their clicks to talk to each other and each pod has its own pattern of clicks and sounds.

The male signals to the others that boats are nearby. The adult whales quickly form a circle around the newborn and three older calves, to protect them.

Dragging behind a fishing boat is a large net with floats attached to the top. The curious newborn breaks out of the circle and heads toward the bright floats. Part of the net that is underwater floats close to one of his flippers and almost catches on it. His mother quickly chases him back to the pod.

This pod is a group of transient or wandering whales that swim all over the oceans. They are heading toward Alaska to hunt during the winter.

As they swim north, they pass another group of whales called resident killer whales. Residents usually stay in the same area for life and feed mostly on fish. When the wanderers pass the residents, some of the females, or cows, breach and loudly slap the water with their flippers. They are sending out mating signals to the resident males.

Soon the wanderers are following a school of salmon swimming toward the shore. Wandering whales usually hunt larger prey like seals and squid, but they will eat fish.

When they get close to the shore of southern Alaska, one whale swims straight up to the surface. His huge head slowly rises out of the water and he lifts the top half of his body completely out of the water. He looks all around, then silently sinks out of sight. This movement is called spyhopping. Back underwater, he sends out a series of fast clicks to tell the others he has spied something.

The group quickly surfaces and swims toward the shore where a group of noisy steller sea lions have gathered close to the water.

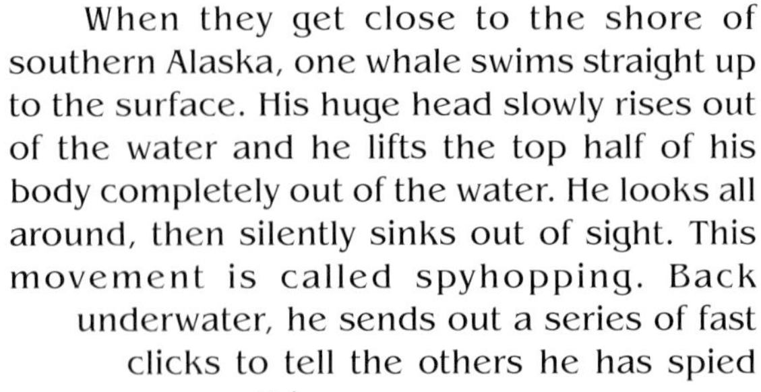

Several of the whales rush toward them and actually swim up onto the ice to try to catch the sea lions. Quickly, the sea lions scamper farther inland, out of the reach of the whales. Frustrated, the whales use their flippers to turn around and slowly wiggle back into the breaking waves.

Tired from their travels and hunting, the whales rest near the shore. Whales do not actually sleep, but only rest on the water's surface. They notice the tide is starting to go out, and rapidly swim toward deeper waters. If they stay in the shallow water when the tide goes out, they would be stranded on the beach.

They continue their journey north. Much of the time they speed-swim on the surface instead of swimming underwater. Along the way, the calves play with each other, leaping high in the air, twisting their bodies and slapping their flippers on the water, creating big splashes.

GLOSSARY TERMS

Blowhole—The hole on the backs of whales that is used for breathing.

Breaching—Leaping out of the water for the purpose of communicating or playing.